JUZ'U 'AMMA

WITH
COLOUR CODED TAJWEED RULES IN ENGLISH

It is a great pleasure for Islamic Book Service New Delhi to introduce this project in India for the first time. This humble effort is an attempt to facilitate the Tilaawah of the Juz'u'Amma with Tajweed.

Seven different colour shades have been used and each colour represents a Tajweed Rule.

The colour coding system has been introduced to highlight the Rules of Tajweed found in the Qurâ'nic text. Having a colour block on the Tajweed Rule allows the reciter to emphasise the accent, phonetics, rhythm and temper of the Qurâ'nic recitation.

It is imperative for the reciter to have a working knowledge of the Rules of Tajweed in order to know how to pronounce the letters on which emphasis has to be laid.

We shall appreciate feedback, if any, on this colour coded concept for the benefit of the reciter.

Islamic Book Service

2872-74 Kucha Chelan, Darya Ganj, New Delhi-110002 **(India)**
Ph.: 23253514, 23286551, 23244556, **Fax:** 011-23277913
E-mail: Islamic@eth.net. lbsdelhi@del2.vsnl.net.in
Website: www.islamic-india.com

COLOUR CODED TAJWEED RULES

Ikhfa

if any one of these letters

ت ث ج د ذ ز س ش ص ض ط ظ ف ق ك

appear after a نْ or _____ it will be pronounced with a light nasal sound.

• Ghunna

The sound emanates from the nose and is observed on the مّ & نّ

Ikhfa Meem Saakin

When the letter ب appears after a مْ it will be pronounced with a light sound in the nose.

Idghaam

If after a نْ or _____ there appear any of these letters (ي ن م و) it will become assimilated into the letter and will be read with Ghunna.

Qalqala

The five letters of Qalqala are ق ط ب ج د .
When any of these letters in a word has a Sukoon on it or if deciding on pausing on any of these letters which appear at the end of a sentence it will appear to have an echoing or jerking sound.

Qalb

If after a نْ or _____ the letter ب appears then the Noon Saakin or Tanween will be incorporated into the letter مْ and will be recited with Ghunna.

Idghaam Meem Saakin

If after a مْ there appear another مْ the two meems will become incorporated and will be read with Ghunna.

بِسۡمِ اللّٰهِ الرَّحۡمٰنِ الرَّحِیۡمِ

سُوْرَةُ النَّاسِ مَكِّيَّةٌ (١١٤) اٰیَاتُهَا ٦ رُكُوْعُهَا ١

بِسْمِ اللّٰهِ الرَّحْمٰنِ الرَّحِيْمِ

قُلْ اَعُوْذُ بِرَبِّ النَّاسِ ۙ١ مَلِكِ النَّاسِ ۙ٢ اِلٰهِ النَّاسِ ۙ٣ مِنْ شَرِّ الْوَسْوَاسِ ۙ۵ الْخَنَّاسِ ۙ٤ الَّذِيْ يُوَسْوِسُ فِيْ صُدُوْرِ النَّاسِ ۙ۵ مِنَ الْجِنَّةِ وَالنَّاسِ ۧ٦

سُوْرَةُ الْفَلَقِ مَكِّيَّةٌ (١١٣) اٰیَاتُهَا ۵ رُكُوْعُهَا ١

بِسْمِ اللّٰهِ الرَّحْمٰنِ الرَّحِيْمِ

قُلْ اَعُوْذُ بِرَبِّ الْفَلَقِ ۙ١ مِنْ شَرِّ مَا خَلَقَ ۙ٢ وَ مِنْ شَرِّ غَاسِقٍ اِذَا وَقَبَ ۙ٣ وَ مِنْ شَرِّ النَّفّٰثٰتِ فِى الْعُقَدِ ۙ٤ وَ مِنْ شَرِّ حَاسِدٍ اِذَا حَسَدَ ۧ۵

سُوْرَةُ الْاِخْلَاصِ مَكِّيَّةٌ (١١٢) اٰیَاتُهَا ٤ رُكُوْعُهَا ١

بِسْمِ اللّٰهِ الرَّحْمٰنِ الرَّحِيْمِ

قُلْ هُوَ اللّٰهُ اَحَدٌ ۚ١ اَللّٰهُ الصَّمَدُ ۚ٢ لَمْ يَلِدْ ۙ۬ وَلَمْ

Ikhfa   Ghunna   Ikhfa Meem Saakin   Idghaam   Qalqala   Qalb   Idghaam Meem Saakin

Ikhfa ◼ Ghunna ◻ Ikhfa Meem Saakin ◼ Idghaam ◻ Qalb ◼ Qalqala ◼ Idghaam Meem Saakin ◼

قُلْ يٰٓاَيُّهَا الْكٰفِرُوْنَ ﴿١﴾ لَآ اَعْبُدُ مَا تَعْبُدُوْنَ ﴿٢﴾ وَلَآ
اَنْتُمْ عٰبِدُوْنَ مَآ اَعْبُدُ ﴿٣﴾ وَلَآ اَنَا عَابِدٌ مَّا عَبَدْتُّمْ ﴿٤﴾ وَلَآ
اَنْتُمْ عٰبِدُوْنَ مَآ اَعْبُدُ ﴿٥﴾ لَكُمْ دِيْنُكُمْ وَلِيَ دِيْنِ ﴿٦﴾ ع ٦ ٣٤

ايَاتُهَا ٣ (١٠٨) سُوْرَةُ الْكَوْثَرِ مَكِّيَّةٌ (١٥) رُكُوْعُهَا ١

بِسْمِ اللّٰهِ الرَّحْمٰنِ الرَّحِيْمِ

اِنَّآ اَعْطَيْنٰكَ الْكَوْثَرَ ﴿١﴾ فَصَلِّ لِرَبِّكَ وَانْحَرْ ﴿٢﴾
اِنَّ شَانِئَكَ هُوَ الْاَبْتَرُ ﴿٣﴾ ع ٣ ٣٣

مَنْزِل ٧

ايَاتُهَا ٧ (١٠٧) سُوْرَةُ الْمَاعُوْنِ مَكِّيَّةٌ (١٧) رُكُوْعُهَا ١

بِسْمِ اللّٰهِ الرَّحْمٰنِ الرَّحِيْمِ

اَرَءَيْتَ الَّذِيْ يُكَذِّبُ بِالدِّيْنِ ﴿١﴾ فَذٰلِكَ الَّذِيْ يَدُعُّ
الْيَتِيْمَ ﴿٢﴾ وَلَا يَحُضُّ عَلٰى طَعَامِ الْمِسْكِيْنِ ﴿٣﴾ فَوَيْلٌ
لِّلْمُصَلِّيْنَ ﴿٤﴾ الَّذِيْنَ هُمْ عَنْ صَلَاتِهِمْ سَاهُوْنَ ﴿٥﴾
الَّذِيْنَ هُمْ يُرَآءُوْنَ ﴿٦﴾ وَيَمْنَعُوْنَ الْمَاعُوْنَ ﴿٧﴾ ع ٧ ٣٢

Ikhfa | Ghunna | Ikhfa Meem Saakin | Idghaam | Qalqala | Qalb | Idghaam Meem Saakin

بِسۡمِ ٱللَّهِ ٱلرَّحۡمَٰنِ ٱلرَّحِيمِ

اَنَّ مَالَهٗۤ اَخۡلَدَهٗ ۚ﴿۳﴾ كَلَّا لَيُنۡۢبَذَنَّ فِى الۡحُطَمَةِ ۖ﴿۴﴾ وَمَاۤ
اَدۡرٰىكَ مَا الۡحُطَمَةُ ؕ﴿۵﴾ نَارُ اللّٰهِ الۡمُوۡقَدَةُ ۙ﴿۶﴾ الَّتِىۡ تَطَّلِعُ
عَلَى الۡاَفۡـِٕدَةِ ؕ﴿۷﴾ اِنَّهَا عَلَيۡهِمۡ مُّؤۡصَدَةٌ ۙ﴿۸﴾ فِىۡ عَمَدٍ مُّمَدَّدَةٍ ﴿۹﴾ ع ٩/٢٩

سُوۡرَةُ الۡعَصۡرِ مَكِّيَّةٌ (١٠٣) (١٣) اٰيَاتُهَا ٣ رُكُوۡعُهَا ١

بِسۡمِ اللّٰهِ الرَّحۡمٰنِ الرَّحِيۡمِ

وَالۡعَصۡرِۙ﴿۱﴾ اِنَّ الۡاِنۡسَانَ لَفِىۡ خُسۡرٍۙ﴿۲﴾ اِلَّا الَّذِيۡنَ اٰمَنُوۡا
وَعَمِلُوا الصّٰلِحٰتِ وَتَوَاصَوۡا بِالۡحَقِّ ۙ وَتَوَاصَوۡا بِالصَّبۡرِ﴿۳﴾ ع ٣/٢٨

منزل ٧

سُوۡرَةُ التَّكَاثُرِ مَكِّيَّةٌ (١٠٢) (١٦) اٰيَاتُهَا ٨ رُكُوۡعُهَا ١

بِسۡمِ اللّٰهِ الرَّحۡمٰنِ الرَّحِيۡمِ

اَلۡهٰٮكُمُ التَّكَاثُرُۙ﴿۱﴾ حَتّٰى زُرۡتُمُ الۡمَقَابِرَؕ﴿۲﴾ كَلَّا سَوۡفَ
تَعۡلَمُوۡنَۙ﴿۳﴾ ثُمَّ كَلَّا سَوۡفَ تَعۡلَمُوۡنَؕ﴿۴﴾ كَلَّا لَوۡ تَعۡلَمُوۡنَ
عِلۡمَ الۡيَقِيۡنِؕ﴿۵﴾ لَتَرَوُنَّ الۡجَحِيۡمَۙ﴿۶﴾ ثُمَّ لَتَرَوُنَّهَا
عَيۡنَ الۡيَقِيۡنِۙ﴿۷﴾ ثُمَّ لَتُسۡـَٔلُنَّ يَوۡمَٮِٕذٍ عَنِ النَّعِيۡمِ﴿۸﴾ ع ٨/٢٧

Ikhfa | Ghunna | Ikhfa Meem Saakin | Idghaam | Qalqala | Qalb | Idghaam Meem Saakin

سُوْرَةُ الْقَارِعَةِ مَكِّيَّةٌ (١٠١) (٣٠)

اٰيَاتُهَا ١١ — رُكُوْعُهَا ١

بِسْمِ اللّٰهِ الرَّحْمٰنِ الرَّحِيْمِ ○

اَلْقَارِعَةُ ① مَا الْقَارِعَةُ ② وَمَآ اَدْرٰىكَ مَا الْقَارِعَةُ ③
يَوْمَ يَكُوْنُ النَّاسُ كَالْفَرَاشِ الْمَبْثُوْثِ ④ وَتَكُوْنُ
الْجِبَالُ كَالْعِهْنِ الْمَنْفُوْشِ ⑤ فَاَمَّا مَنْ ثَقُلَتْ مَوَازِيْنُهٗ ⑥
فَهُوَ فِيْ عِيْشَةٍ رَّاضِيَةٍ ⑦ وَاَمَّا مَنْ خَفَّتْ مَوَازِيْنُهٗ ⑧
فَاُمُّهٗ هَاوِيَةٌ ⑨ وَمَآ اَدْرٰىكَ مَا هِيَهْ ⑩ نَارٌ حَامِيَةٌ ⑪

سُوْرَةُ الْعٰدِيٰتِ مَكِّيَّةٌ (١٠٠) (١٤)

اٰيَاتُهَا ١١ — رُكُوْعُهَا ١

بِسْمِ اللّٰهِ الرَّحْمٰنِ الرَّحِيْمِ ○

وَالْعٰدِيٰتِ ضَبْحًا ① فَالْمُوْرِيٰتِ قَدْحًا ② فَالْمُغِيْرٰتِ
صُبْحًا ③ فَاَثَرْنَ بِهٖ نَقْعًا ④ فَوَسَطْنَ بِهٖ جَمْعًا ⑤
اِنَّ الْاِنْسَانَ لِرَبِّهٖ لَكَنُوْدٌ ⑥ وَاِنَّهٗ عَلٰى
ذٰلِكَ لَشَهِيْدٌ ⑦ وَاِنَّهٗ لِحُبِّ الْخَيْرِ لَشَدِيْدٌ ⑧

منزل ٧ — ع ١١/٢٦

Ikhfa | Ghunna | Ikhfa Meem Saakin | Idghaam | Qalqala | Qalb | Idghaam Meem Saakin

اَفَلَا يَعْلَمُ اِذَا بُعْثِرَ مَا فِي الْقُبُوْرِ ﴿٩﴾ وَحُصِّلَ

مَا فِي الصُّدُوْرِ ﴿١٠﴾ اِنَّ رَبَّهُمْ بِهِمْ يَوْمَئِذٍ

ع ١١/٢٥ لَّخَبِيْرٌ ﴿١١﴾

رُكُوعُهَا ١ (٩٩) سُوْرَةُ الزِّلْزَالِ مَدَنِيَّةٌ (٩٣) اٰيَاتُهَا ٨

بِسْمِ اللّٰهِ الرَّحْمٰنِ الرَّحِيْمِ

اِذَا زُلْزِلَتِ الْاَرْضُ زِلْزَالَهَا ﴿١﴾ وَاَخْرَجَتِ الْاَرْضُ

اَثْقَالَهَا ﴿٢﴾ وَقَالَ الْاِنْسَانُ مَا لَهَا ﴿٣﴾ يَوْمَئِذٍ تُحَدِّثُ منزل ٧

اَخْبَارَهَا ﴿٤﴾ بِاَنَّ رَبَّكَ اَوْحٰى لَهَا ﴿٥﴾ يَوْمَئِذٍ يَّصْدُرُ النَّاسُ

اَشْتَاتًا ۙ لِّيُرَوْا اَعْمَالَهُمْ ﴿٦﴾ فَمَنْ يَّعْمَلْ مِثْقَالَ ذَرَّةٍ

ع ٨/٢٤ خَيْرًا يَّرَهٗ ﴿٧﴾ وَمَنْ يَّعْمَلْ مِثْقَالَ ذَرَّةٍ شَرًّا يَّرَهٗ ﴿٨﴾

رُكُوعُهَا ١ (٩٨) سُوْرَةُ الْبَيِّنَةِ مَدَنِيَّةٌ (١٠٠) اٰيَاتُهَا ٨

بِسْمِ اللّٰهِ الرَّحْمٰنِ الرَّحِيْمِ

لَمْ يَكُنِ الَّذِيْنَ كَفَرُوْا مِنْ اَهْلِ الْكِتٰبِ وَالْمُشْرِكِيْنَ مُنْفَكِّيْنَ

Ikhfa | Ghunna | Ikhfa Meem Saakin | Idghaam | Qalqala | Qalb | Idghaam Meem Saakin

حَتّٰى تَأْتِيَهُمُ الْبَيِّنَةُ ۙ ﴿١﴾ رَسُوْلٌ مِّنَ اللّٰهِ يَتْلُوْا صُحُفًا مُّطَهَّرَةً ۙ ﴿٢﴾
فِيْهَا كُتُبٌ قَيِّمَةٌ ؕ ﴿٣﴾ وَمَا تَفَرَّقَ الَّذِيْنَ اُوْتُوا الْكِتٰبَ
اِلَّا مِنْۢ بَعْدِ مَا جَآءَتْهُمُ الْبَيِّنَةُ ؕ ﴿٤﴾ وَمَآ اُمِرُوْٓا اِلَّا
لِيَعْبُدُوا اللّٰهَ مُخْلِصِيْنَ لَهُ الدِّيْنَ ۙ۬ حُنَفَآءَ وَيُقِيْمُوا
الصَّلٰوةَ وَيُؤْتُوا الزَّكٰوةَ وَذٰلِكَ دِيْنُ الْقَيِّمَةِ ؕ ﴿٥﴾ اِنَّ الَّذِيْنَ
كَفَرُوْا مِنْ اَهْلِ الْكِتٰبِ وَالْمُشْرِكِيْنَ فِيْ نَارِ جَهَنَّمَ خٰلِدِيْنَ
منزل ٧ فِيْهَا ؕ اُولٰٓئِكَ هُمْ شَرُّ الْبَرِيَّةِ ؕ ﴿٦﴾ اِنَّ الَّذِيْنَ اٰمَنُوْا وَعَمِلُوا
الصّٰلِحٰتِ ۙ اُولٰٓئِكَ هُمْ خَيْرُ الْبَرِيَّةِ ؕ ﴿٧﴾ جَزَآؤُهُمْ عِنْدَ رَبِّهِمْ
جَنّٰتُ عَدْنٍ تَجْرِيْ مِنْ تَحْتِهَا الْاَنْهٰرُ خٰلِدِيْنَ فِيْهَآ اَبَدًا ؕ
رَضِيَ اللّٰهُ عَنْهُمْ وَرَضُوْا عَنْهُ ؕ ذٰلِكَ لِمَنْ خَشِيَ رَبَّهٗ ع ﴿٨﴾ ع ٨ ٢٣

اٰيَاتُهَا ٥ — سُوْرَةُ الْقَدْرِ مَكِّيَّةٌ (٩٧) (٢٥) — رُكُوْعُهَا ١

بِسْمِ اللّٰهِ الرَّحْمٰنِ الرَّحِيْمِ ۝

اِنَّآ اَنْزَلْنٰهُ فِيْ لَيْلَةِ الْقَدْرِ ۚۖ ﴿١﴾ وَمَآ اَدْرٰىكَ مَا لَيْلَةُ الْقَدْرِ ؕ ﴿٢﴾

لَيْلَةُ الْقَدْرِ ۙۥ خَيْرٌ مِّنْ اَلْفِ شَهْرٍ ۝٣ؕ تَنَزَّلُ الْمَلٰٓئِكَةُ وَالرُّوْحُ

فِيْهَا بِاِذْنِ رَبِّهِمْ مِّنْ كُلِّ اَمْرٍ ۝٤ۛ سَلٰمٌ ۛ قف هِيَ حَتّٰى مَطْلَعِ الْفَجْرِ ۝٥ ع

ايَاتُهَا ١٩ (٩٦) سُوْرَةُ الْعَلَقِ مَكِّيَّةٌ (١) رُكُوعُهَا ١

بِسْمِ اللّٰهِ الرَّحْمٰنِ الرَّحِيْمِ ○

اِقْرَاْ بِاسْمِ رَبِّكَ الَّذِيْ خَلَقَ ۝١ۚ خَلَقَ الْاِنْسَانَ مِنْ

عَلَقٍ ۝٢ۚ اِقْرَاْ وَرَبُّكَ الْاَكْرَمُ ۝٣ۙ الَّذِيْ عَلَّمَ بِالْقَلَمِ ۝٤ۙ

عَلَّمَ الْاِنْسَانَ مَا لَمْ يَعْلَمْ ۝٥ؕ كَلَّآ اِنَّ الْاِنْسَانَ لَيَطْغٰٓى ۝٦ۙ

اَنْ رَّاٰهُ اسْتَغْنٰى ۝٧ؕ اِنَّ اِلٰى رَبِّكَ الرُّجْعٰى ۝٨ؕ اَرَءَيْتَ الَّذِيْ

يَنْهٰى ۝٩ۙ عَبْدًا اِذَا صَلّٰى ۝١٠ؕ اَرَءَيْتَ اِنْ كَانَ عَلَى

الْهُدٰٓى ۝١١ۙ اَوْ اَمَرَ بِالتَّقْوٰى ۝١٢ؕ اَرَءَيْتَ اِنْ كَذَّبَ وَتَوَلّٰى ۝١٣ؕ

اَلَمْ يَعْلَمْ بِاَنَّ اللّٰهَ يَرٰى ۝١٤ؕ كَلَّا لَئِنْ لَّمْ يَنْتَهِ ۙۥ لَنَسْفَعًۢا

بِالنَّاصِيَةِ ۝١٥ۙ نَاصِيَةٍ كَاذِبَةٍ خَاطِئَةٍ ۝١٦ۚ فَلْيَدْعُ نَادِيَهٗ ۝١٧ۙ

سَنَدْعُ الزَّبَانِيَةَ ۝١٨ۙ كَلَّا ؕ لَا تُطِعْهُ وَاسْجُدْ وَاقْتَرِبْ ۝١٩ ع السجدة

منزل ٧

Ikhfa | Ghunna | Ikhfa Meem Saakin | Idghaam | Qalqala | Qalb | Idghaam Meem Saakin

بِسْمِ اللَّهِ الرَّحْمَٰنِ الرَّحِيمِ

بِسْمِ اللَّهِ الرَّحْمَٰنِ الرَّحِيمِ

اٰیاتُها ١١ (٩٣) سُوْرَةُ الضُّحٰى مَكِّيَّةٌ (١١) رُكُوعُها ١

بِسْمِ اللّٰهِ الرَّحْمٰنِ الرَّحِيْمِ

وَالضُّحٰى ﴿١﴾ وَالَّيْلِ اِذَا سَجٰى ﴿٢﴾ مَا وَدَّعَكَ رَبُّكَ وَمَا قَلٰى ﴿٣﴾ وَ
لَلْاٰخِرَةُ خَيْرٌ لَّكَ مِنَ الْاُوْلٰى ﴿٤﴾ وَلَسَوْفَ يُعْطِيْكَ رَبُّكَ
فَتَرْضٰى ﴿٥﴾ اَلَمْ يَجِدْكَ يَتِيْمًا فَاٰوٰى ﴿٦﴾ وَوَجَدَكَ ضَآلًّا
فَهَدٰى ﴿٧﴾ وَوَجَدَكَ عَآئِلًا فَاَغْنٰى ﴿٨﴾ فَاَمَّا الْيَتِيْمَ فَلَا
تَقْهَرْ ﴿٩﴾ وَاَمَّا السَّآئِلَ فَلَا تَنْهَرْ ﴿١٠﴾ وَاَمَّا بِنِعْمَةِ رَبِّكَ فَحَدِّثْ ﴿١١﴾ ع ١١/١٨

منزل ٧

اٰیاتُها ٢١ (٩٢) سُوْرَةُ الَّيْلِ مَكِّيَّةٌ (٩) رُكُوعُها ١

بِسْمِ اللّٰهِ الرَّحْمٰنِ الرَّحِيْمِ

وَالَّيْلِ اِذَا يَغْشٰى ﴿١﴾ وَالنَّهَارِ اِذَا تَجَلّٰى ﴿٢﴾ وَمَا خَلَقَ
الذَّكَرَ وَالْاُنْثٰٓى ﴿٣﴾ اِنَّ سَعْيَكُمْ لَشَتّٰى ﴿٤﴾ فَاَمَّا مَنْ اَعْطٰى
وَاتَّقٰى ﴿٥﴾ وَصَدَّقَ بِالْحُسْنٰى ﴿٦﴾ فَسَنُيَسِّرُهٗ لِلْيُسْرٰى ﴿٧﴾ وَ
اَمَّا مَنْ بَخِلَ وَاسْتَغْنٰى ﴿٨﴾ وَكَذَّبَ بِالْحُسْنٰى ﴿٩﴾ فَسَنُيَسِّرُهٗ

Ikhfa | Ghunna | Ikhfa Meem Saakin | Idghaam | Qalqala | Qalb | Idghaam Meem Saakin

بسم الله الرحمن الرحيم

ثُمَّ كَانَ مِنَ الَّذِينَ اٰمَنُوْا وَتَوَاصَوْا بِالصَّبْرِ وَتَوَاصَوْا بِالْمَرْحَمَةِ ۞

اُولٰٓئِكَ اَصْحٰبُ الْمَيْمَنَةِ ۞ وَالَّذِيْنَ كَفَرُوْا بِاٰيٰتِنَا

هُمْ اَصْحٰبُ الْمَشْـَٔمَةِ ۞ عَلَيْهِمْ نَارٌ مُّؤْصَدَةٌ ۞

سُوْرَةُ الْفَجْرِ مَكِّيَّةٌ (٨٩) اٰيَاتُهَا ٣٠ رُكُوْعُهَا ١

بِسْمِ اللّٰهِ الرَّحْمٰنِ الرَّحِيْمِ ۞

وَالْفَجْرِ ۞ وَلَيَالٍ عَشْرٍ ۞ وَّالشَّفْعِ وَالْوَتْرِ ۞ وَالَّيْلِ اِذَا

يَسْرِ ۞ هَلْ فِيْ ذٰلِكَ قَسَمٌ لِّذِيْ حِجْرٍ ۞ اَلَمْ تَرَ كَيْفَ

فَعَلَ رَبُّكَ بِعَادٍ ۞ اِرَمَ ذَاتِ الْعِمَادِ ۞ الَّتِيْ لَمْ يُخْلَقْ

مِثْلُهَا فِى الْبِلَادِ ۞ وَثَمُوْدَ الَّذِيْنَ جَابُوا الصَّخْرَ بِالْوَادِ ۞

وَفِرْعَوْنَ ذِى الْاَوْتَادِ ۞ الَّذِيْنَ طَغَوْا فِى الْبِلَادِ ۞

فَاَكْثَرُوْا فِيْهَا الْفَسَادَ ۞ فَصَبَّ عَلَيْهِمْ رَبُّكَ سَوْطَ

عَذَابٍ ۞ اِنَّ رَبَّكَ لَبِالْمِرْصَادِ ۞ فَاَمَّا الْاِنْسَانُ اِذَا

مَا ابْتَلٰىهُ رَبُّهٗ فَاَكْرَمَهٗ وَنَعَّمَهٗ ۙ فَيَقُوْلُ رَبِّيْ اَكْرَمَنِ ۞

Ikhfa	Ghunna	Ikhfa Meem Saakin	Idghaam	Qalqala	Qalb	Idghaam Meem Saakin

وَأَمَّآ إِذَا مَا ابْتَلٰىهُ فَقَدَرَ عَلَيْهِ رِزْقَهٗ ۥ فَيَقُولُ رَبِّيٓ
أَهَانَنِ ﴿١٦﴾ كَلَّا بَل لَّا تُكْرِمُونَ الْيَتِيمَ ﴿١٧﴾ وَلَا تَحَٰٓضُّونَ
عَلٰى طَعَامِ الْمِسْكِينِ ﴿١٨﴾ وَتَأْكُلُونَ التُّرَاثَ أَكْلًا لَّمًّا ﴿١٩﴾
وَتُحِبُّونَ الْمَالَ حُبًّا جَمًّا ﴿٢٠﴾ كَلَّآ إِذَا دُكَّتِ الْأَرْضُ دَكًّا
دَكًّا ﴿٢١﴾ وَجَآءَ رَبُّكَ وَالْمَلَكُ صَفًّا صَفًّا ﴿٢٢﴾ وَجِاىٓءَ يَوْمَئِذٍۢ
بِجَهَنَّمَ ۥ يَوْمَئِذٍ يَتَذَكَّرُ الْإِنسَانُ وَأَنّٰى لَهُ الذِّكْرٰى ﴿٢٣﴾
يَقُولُ يٰلَيْتَنِى قَدَّمْتُ لِحَيَاتِى ﴿٢٤﴾ فَيَوْمَئِذٍ لَّا يُعَذِّبُ
عَذَابَهٗٓ أَحَدٌ ﴿٢٥﴾ وَلَا يُوثِقُ وَثَاقَهٗٓ أَحَدٌ ﴿٢٦﴾ يٰٓأَيَّتُهَا
النَّفْسُ الْمُطْمَئِنَّةُ ﴿٢٧﴾ ارْجِعِىٓ إِلٰى رَبِّكِ رَاضِيَةً مَّرْضِيَّةً ﴿٢٨﴾
فَادْخُلِى فِى عِبٰدِى ﴿٢٩﴾ وَادْخُلِى جَنَّتِى ﴿٣٠﴾

آيَاتُهَا ٢٦ (٨٨) سُورَةُ الْغَاشِيَةِ مَكِّيَّةٌ (٦٨) رُكُوعُهَا ١

بِسْمِ اللّٰهِ الرَّحْمٰنِ الرَّحِيمِ

هَلْ أَتٰىكَ حَدِيثُ الْغَاشِيَةِ ﴿١﴾ وُجُوهٌ يَوْمَئِذٍ خَاشِعَةٌ ﴿٢﴾

منزل ٧

ع ١٤

Ikhfa | Ghunna | Ikhfa Meem Saakin | Idghaam | Qalqala | Qalb | Idghaam Meem Saakin

بِسْمِ اللَّهِ الرَّحْمَٰنِ الرَّحِيمِ

وَالْمُرْسَلَاتِ عُرْفًا ۝ فَالْعَاصِفَاتِ عَصْفًا ۝ وَالنَّاشِرَاتِ نَشْرًا ۝ فَالْفَارِقَاتِ فَرْقًا ۝ فَالْمُلْقِيَاتِ ذِكْرًا ۝ عُذْرًا أَوْ نُذْرًا ۝ إِنَّمَا تُوعَدُونَ لَوَاقِعٌ ۝

فَإِذَا النُّجُومُ طُمِسَتْ ۝ وَإِذَا السَّمَاءُ فُرِجَتْ ۝ وَإِذَا الْجِبَالُ نُسِفَتْ ۝ وَإِذَا الرُّسُلُ أُقِّتَتْ ۝ لِأَيِّ يَوْمٍ أُجِّلَتْ ۝ لِيَوْمِ الْفَصْلِ ۝ وَمَا أَدْرَاكَ مَا يَوْمُ الْفَصْلِ ۝ وَيْلٌ يَوْمَئِذٍ لِلْمُكَذِّبِينَ ۝

أَلَمْ نُهْلِكِ الْأَوَّلِينَ ۝ ثُمَّ نُتْبِعُهُمُ الْآخِرِينَ ۝ كَذَٰلِكَ نَفْعَلُ بِالْمُجْرِمِينَ ۝ وَيْلٌ يَوْمَئِذٍ لِلْمُكَذِّبِينَ ۝ أَلَمْ نَخْلُقْكُمْ مِنْ مَاءٍ مَهِينٍ ۝ فَجَعَلْنَاهُ فِي قَرَارٍ مَكِينٍ ۝ إِلَىٰ قَدَرٍ مَعْلُومٍ ۝ فَقَدَرْنَا فَنِعْمَ الْقَادِرُونَ ۝ وَيْلٌ يَوْمَئِذٍ لِلْمُكَذِّبِينَ ۝

أَلَمْ نَجْعَلِ الْأَرْضَ كِفَاتًا ۝ أَحْيَاءً وَأَمْوَاتًا ۝ وَجَعَلْنَا فِيهَا رَوَاسِيَ شَامِخَاتٍ وَأَسْقَيْنَاكُمْ مَاءً فُرَاتًا ۝ وَيْلٌ يَوْمَئِذٍ لِلْمُكَذِّبِينَ ۝

آیاتُها ١٩ (٨٧) سُوْرَةُ الْاَعْلٰى مَكِّيَّةٌ (٨) رُكُوعُهَا ١

بِسْمِ اللّٰهِ الرَّحْمٰنِ الرَّحِیْمِ ○

سَبِّحِ اسْمَ رَبِّكَ الْاَعْلَى ۝١ الَّذِیْ خَلَقَ فَسَوّٰی ۝٢
وَالَّذِیْ قَدَّرَ فَهَدٰی ۝٣ وَالَّذِیْٓ اَخْرَجَ الْمَرْعٰی ۝٤
فَجَعَلَهٗ غُثَآءً اَحْوٰی ۝٥ سَنُقْرِئُكَ فَلَا تَنْسٰٓی ۝٦ اِلَّا
مَا شَآءَ اللّٰهُ ؕ اِنَّهٗ یَعْلَمُ الْجَهْرَ وَمَا یَخْفٰی ۝٧ وَنُیَسِّرُكَ
لِلْیُسْرٰی ۝٨ فَذَكِّرْ اِنْ نَّفَعَتِ الذِّكْرٰی ۝٩
سَیَذَّكَّرُ مَنْ یَّخْشٰی ۝١٠ وَیَتَجَنَّبُهَا الْاَشْقَی ۝١١ الَّذِیْ
یَصْلَی النَّارَ الْكُبْرٰی ۝١٢ ثُمَّ لَا یَمُوْتُ فِیْهَا وَلَا یَحْیٰی ۝١٣
قَدْ اَفْلَحَ مَنْ تَزَكّٰی ۝١٤ وَذَكَرَ اسْمَ رَبِّهٖ فَصَلّٰی ۝١٥ بَلْ
تُؤْثِرُوْنَ الْحَیٰوةَ الدُّنْیَا ۝١٦ وَالْاٰخِرَةُ خَیْرٌ وَّاَبْقٰی ۝١٧
اِنَّ هٰذَا لَفِی الصُّحُفِ الْاُوْلٰی ۝١٨ صُحُفِ اِبْرٰهِیْمَ
وَمُوْسٰی ۝١٩ ع

منزل ٧

ع ١٩/١٢ ١

Ikhfa · Ghunna · Ikhfa Meem Saakin · Idghaam · Qalqala · Qalb · Idghaam Meem Saakin

اٰيَاتُهَا ١٧ (٨٦) سُوْرَةُ الطَّارِقِ مَكِّيَّةٌ (٣٦) رُكُوْعُهَا ١

بِسْمِ اللّٰهِ الرَّحْمٰنِ الرَّحِيْمِ ○

وَالسَّمَآءِ وَالطَّارِقِ ﴿١﴾ وَمَآ اَدْرٰىكَ مَا الطَّارِقُ ﴿٢﴾ النَّجْمُ
الثَّاقِبُ ﴿٣﴾ اِنْ كُلُّ نَفْسٍ لَّمَّا عَلَيْهَا حَافِظٌ ﴿٤﴾ فَلْيَنْظُرِ
الْاِنْسَانُ مِمَّ خُلِقَ ﴿٥﴾ خُلِقَ مِنْ مَّآءٍ دَافِقٍ ﴿٦﴾ يَّخْرُجُ مِنْۢ
بَيْنِ الصُّلْبِ وَالتَّرَآئِبِ ﴿٧﴾ اِنَّهٗ عَلٰى رَجْعِهٖ لَقَادِرٌ ﴿٨﴾
يَوْمَ تُبْلَى السَّرَآئِرُ ﴿٩﴾ فَمَا لَهٗ مِنْ قُوَّةٍ وَّلَا نَاصِرٍ ﴿١٠﴾ وَالسَّمَآءِ
ذَاتِ الرَّجْعِ ﴿١١﴾ وَالْاَرْضِ ذَاتِ الصَّدْعِ ﴿١٢﴾ اِنَّهٗ لَقَوْلٌ
فَصْلٌ ﴿١٣﴾ وَّمَا هُوَ بِالْهَزْلِ ﴿١٤﴾ اِنَّهُمْ يَكِيْدُوْنَ كَيْدًا ﴿١٥﴾
وَّاَكِيْدُ كَيْدًا ﴿١٦﴾ فَمَهِّلِ الْكٰفِرِيْنَ اَمْهِلْهُمْ رُوَيْدًا ﴿١٧﴾ ع ١٧/١١

منزل ٧

اٰيَاتُهَا ٢٢ (٨٥) سُوْرَةُ الْبُرُوْجِ مَكِّيَّةٌ (٢٧) رُكُوْعُهَا ١

بِسْمِ اللّٰهِ الرَّحْمٰنِ الرَّحِيْمِ ○

وَالسَّمَآءِ ذَاتِ الْبُرُوْجِ ﴿١﴾ وَالْيَوْمِ الْمَوْعُوْدِ ﴿٢﴾ وَشَاهِدٍ

Ikhfa | Ghunna | Ikhfa Meem Saakin | Idghaam | Qalqala | Qalb | Idghaam Meem Saakin

وَّمَشْهُوْدٍ ﴿٣﴾ قُتِلَ اَصْحٰبُ الْاُخْدُوْدِ ﴿٤﴾ النَّارِ ذَاتِ
الْوَقُوْدِ ﴿٥﴾ اِذْ هُمْ عَلَيْهَا قُعُوْدٌ ﴿٦﴾ وَّهُمْ عَلٰى مَا يَفْعَلُوْنَ
بِالْمُؤْمِنِيْنَ شُهُوْدٌ ﴿٧﴾ وَمَا نَقَمُوْا مِنْهُمْ اِلَّآ اَنْ يُّؤْمِنُوْا
بِاللّٰهِ الْعَزِيْزِ الْحَمِيْدِ ﴿٨﴾ الَّذِيْ لَهٗ مُلْكُ السَّمٰوٰتِ وَالْاَرْضِ
وَاللّٰهُ عَلٰى كُلِّ شَيْءٍ شَهِيْدٌ ﴿٩﴾ اِنَّ الَّذِيْنَ فَتَنُوا الْمُؤْمِنِيْنَ
وَالْمُؤْمِنٰتِ ثُمَّ لَمْ يَتُوْبُوْا فَلَهُمْ عَذَابُ جَهَنَّمَ وَلَهُمْ عَذَابُ
الْحَرِيْقِ ﴿١٠﴾ اِنَّ الَّذِيْنَ اٰمَنُوْا وَعَمِلُوا الصّٰلِحٰتِ لَهُمْ جَنّٰتٌ
تَجْرِيْ مِنْ تَحْتِهَا الْاَنْهٰرُ ۬ؕ ذٰلِكَ الْفَوْزُ الْكَبِيْرُ ﴿١١﴾ اِنَّ
بَطْشَ رَبِّكَ لَشَدِيْدٌ ﴿١٢﴾ اِنَّهٗ هُوَ يُبْدِئُ وَيُعِيْدُ ﴿١٣﴾ وَهُوَ
الْغَفُوْرُ الْوَدُوْدُ ﴿١٤﴾ ذُو الْعَرْشِ الْمَجِيْدُ ﴿١٥﴾ فَعَّالٌ لِّمَا
يُرِيْدُ ﴿١٦﴾ هَلْ اَتٰىكَ حَدِيْثُ الْجُنُوْدِ ﴿١٧﴾ فِرْعَوْنَ وَثَمُوْدَ ﴿١٨﴾
بَلِ الَّذِيْنَ كَفَرُوْا فِيْ تَكْذِيْبٍ ﴿١٩﴾ وَّاللّٰهُ مِنْ وَّرَآئِهِمْ
مُّحِيْطٌ ﴿٢٠﴾ بَلْ هُوَ قُرْاٰنٌ مَّجِيْدٌ ﴿٢١﴾ فِيْ لَوْحٍ مَّحْفُوْظٍ ﴿٢٢﴾

منزل ٧

ع ٢٢ ١٠

Ikhfa | Ghunna | Ikhfa Meem Saakin | Idghaam | Qalqala | Qalb | Idghaam Meem Saakin

اٰيَاتُهَا ٢٥ (٨٤) سُوْرَةُ الْاِنْشِقَاقِ مَكِّيَّةٌ (٨٣) رُكُوْعُهَا ١

بِسْمِ اللّٰهِ الرَّحْمٰنِ الرَّحِيْمِ ○

اِذَا السَّمَآءُ انْشَقَّتْ ۙ﴿١﴾ وَاَذِنَتْ لِرَبِّهَا وَحُقَّتْ ۙ﴿٢﴾ وَاِذَا

الْاَرْضُ مُدَّتْ ۙ﴿٣﴾ وَاَلْقَتْ مَا فِيْهَا وَتَخَلَّتْ ۙ﴿٤﴾ وَاَذِنَتْ

لِرَبِّهَا وَحُقَّتْ ؕ﴿٥﴾ يٰاَيُّهَا الْاِنْسَانُ اِنَّكَ كَادِحٌ اِلٰى رَبِّكَ

كَدْحًا فَمُلٰقِيْهِ ۚ﴿٦﴾ فَاَمَّا مَنْ اُوْتِيَ كِتٰبَهٗ بِيَمِيْنِهٖ ۙ﴿٧﴾

فَسَوْفَ يُحَاسَبُ حِسَابًا يَّسِيْرًا ۙ﴿٨﴾ وَّيَنْقَلِبُ اِلٰٓى اَهْلِهٖ

مَسْرُوْرًا ؕ﴿٩﴾ وَاَمَّا مَنْ اُوْتِيَ كِتٰبَهٗ وَرَآءَ ظَهْرِهٖ ۙ﴿١٠﴾ فَسَوْفَ

يَدْعُوْا ثُبُوْرًا ۙ﴿١١﴾ وَّيَصْلٰى سَعِيْرًا ؕ﴿١٢﴾ اِنَّهٗ كَانَ فِيْٓ اَهْلِهٖ

مَسْرُوْرًا ؕ﴿١٣﴾ اِنَّهٗ ظَنَّ اَنْ لَّنْ يَّحُوْرَ ۛۚ﴿١٤﴾ بَلٰٓى ۛۚ اِنَّ رَبَّهٗ كَانَ

بِهٖ بَصِيْرًا ؕ﴿١٥﴾ فَلَآ اُقْسِمُ بِالشَّفَقِ ۙ﴿١٦﴾ وَالَّيْلِ وَمَا

وَسَقَ ۙ﴿١٧﴾ وَالْقَمَرِ اِذَا اتَّسَقَ ۙ﴿١٨﴾ لَتَرْكَبُنَّ طَبَقًا عَنْ طَبَقٍ ؕ﴿١٩﴾

فَمَا لَهُمْ لَا يُؤْمِنُوْنَ ۙ﴿٢٠﴾ وَاِذَا قُرِئَ عَلَيْهِمُ الْقُرْاٰنُ

منزل ٧

معانقة ١٢ عند المتاخرين ١٢

Ikhfa | Ghunna | Ikhfa Meem Saakin | Idghaam | Qalqala | Qalb | Idghaam Meem Saakin

سورة السجدة

مثال ٧

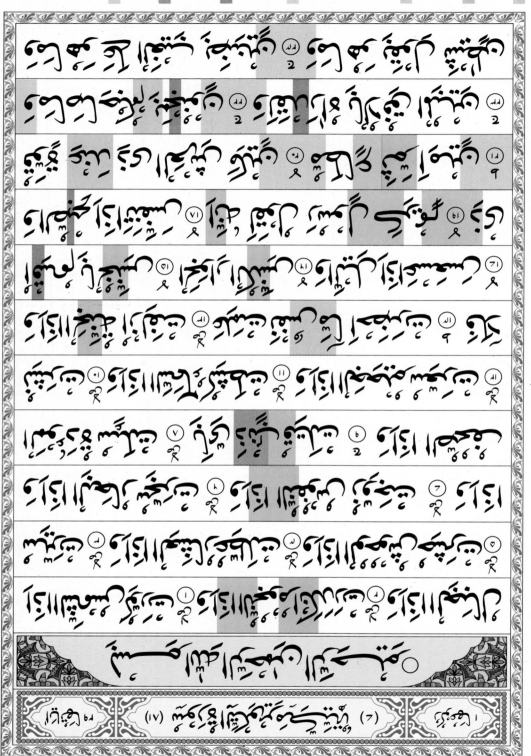

ثُمَّ اِذَا شَآءَ اَنْشَرَهٗ ؕ﴿٢٢﴾ كَلَّا لَمَّا يَقْضِ مَآ اَمَرَهٗ ؕ﴿٢٣﴾ فَلْيَنْظُرِ

الْاِنْسَانُ اِلٰى طَعَامِهٖۤ ۙ﴿٢٤﴾ اَنَّا صَبَبْنَا الْمَآءَ صَبًّا ۙ﴿٢٥﴾ ثُمَّ شَقَقْنَا

الْاَرْضَ شَقًّا ۙ﴿٢٦﴾ فَاَنْۢبَتْنَا فِيْهَا حَبًّا ۙ﴿٢٧﴾ وَّعِنَبًا وَّقَضْبًا ۙ﴿٢٨﴾

وَّزَيْتُوْنًا وَّنَخْلًا ۙ﴿٢٩﴾ وَّحَدَآئِقَ غُلْبًا ۙ﴿٣٠﴾ وَّفَاكِهَةً وَّاَبًّا ۙ﴿٣١﴾

مَّتَاعًا لَّكُمْ وَلِاَنْعَامِكُمْ ؕ﴿٣٢﴾ فَاِذَا جَآءَتِ الصَّآخَّةُ ۫﴿٣٣﴾

يَوْمَ يَفِرُّ الْمَرْءُ مِنْ اَخِيْهِ ۙ﴿٣٤﴾ وَاُمِّهٖ وَاَبِيْهِ ۙ﴿٣٥﴾ وَصَاحِبَتِهٖ

وَبَنِيْهِ ؕ﴿٣٦﴾ لِكُلِّ امْرِئٍ مِّنْهُمْ يَوْمَئِذٍ شَاْنٌ يُّغْنِيْهِ ؕ﴿٣٧﴾

وُجُوْهٌ يَّوْمَئِذٍ مُّسْفِرَةٌ ۙ﴿٣٨﴾ ضَاحِكَةٌ مُّسْتَبْشِرَةٌ ۚ﴿٣٩﴾

وَوُجُوْهٌ يَّوْمَئِذٍ عَلَيْهَا غَبَرَةٌ ۙ﴿٤٠﴾ تَرْهَقُهَا قَتَرَةٌ ؕ﴿٤١﴾

اُولٰٓئِكَ هُمُ الْكَفَرَةُ الْفَجَرَةُ ؏﴿٤٢﴾ ع ١ ٤٢ ٥

اٰيَاتُهَا ٤٦ (٧٩) سُوْرَةُ النّٰزِعٰتِ مَكِّيَّةٌ (٨١) رُكُوْعَاتُهَا ٢

بِسْمِ اللّٰهِ الرَّحْمٰنِ الرَّحِيْمِ

وَالنّٰزِعٰتِ غَرْقًا ۙ﴿١﴾ وَّالنّٰشِطٰتِ نَشْطًا ۙ﴿٢﴾ وَّالسّٰبِحٰتِ

منزل ٧

Ikhfa | Ghunna | Ikhfa Meem Saakin | Idghaam | Qalqala | Qalb | Idghaam Meem Saakin

الأنفال ٨

فَسَوّٰىهَا ﴿٢٨﴾ وَاَغْطَشَ لَيْلَهَا وَاَخْرَجَ ضُحٰىهَا ﴿٢٩﴾ وَالْاَرْضَ بَعْدَ
ذٰلِكَ دَحٰىهَا ﴿٣٠﴾ اَخْرَجَ مِنْهَا مَآءَهَا وَمَرْعٰىهَا ﴿٣١﴾ وَالْجِبَالَ
اَرْسٰىهَا ﴿٣٢﴾ مَتَاعًا لَّكُمْ وَلِاَنْعَامِكُمْ ﴿٣٣﴾ فَاِذَا جَآءَتِ الطَّآمَّةُ
الْكُبْرٰى ﴿٣٤﴾ يَوْمَ يَتَذَكَّرُ الْاِنْسَانُ مَا سَعٰى ﴿٣٥﴾ وَبُرِّزَتِ الْجَحِيْمُ
لِمَنْ يَّرٰى ﴿٣٦﴾ فَاَمَّا مَنْ طَغٰى ﴿٣٧﴾ وَاٰثَرَ الْحَيٰوةَ الدُّنْيَا ﴿٣٨﴾ فَاِنَّ
الْجَحِيْمَ هِيَ الْمَاْوٰى ﴿٣٩﴾ وَاَمَّا مَنْ خَافَ مَقَامَ رَبِّهٖ وَنَهَى
النَّفْسَ عَنِ الْهَوٰى ﴿٤٠﴾ فَاِنَّ الْجَنَّةَ هِيَ الْمَاْوٰى ﴿٤١﴾ يَسْـَٔلُوْنَكَ
عَنِ السَّاعَةِ اَيَّانَ مُرْسٰىهَا ﴿٤٢﴾ فِيْمَ اَنْتَ مِنْ ذِكْرٰىهَا ﴿٤٣﴾
اِلٰى رَبِّكَ مُنْتَهٰىهَا ﴿٤٤﴾ اِنَّمَآ اَنْتَ مُنْذِرُ مَنْ يَّخْشٰىهَا ﴿٤٥﴾
كَاَنَّهُمْ يَوْمَ يَرَوْنَهَا لَمْ يَلْبَثُوْٓا اِلَّا عَشِيَّةً اَوْ ضُحٰىهَا ﴿٤٦﴾ ع

اٰيَاتُهَا ٤٠ — (٧٨) سُوْرَةُ النَّبَا مَكِّيَّةٌ (٨٠) — رُكُوْعَاتُهَا ٢

بِسْمِ اللّٰهِ الرَّحْمٰنِ الرَّحِيْمِ

عَمَّ يَتَسَآءَلُوْنَ ﴿١﴾ عَنِ النَّبَاِ الْعَظِيْمِ ﴿٢﴾ الَّذِيْ هُمْ فِيْهِ

منزل ٧ — ع٢٠ — الجزء الثلثون (٣٠)

Ikhfa · Ghunna · Ikhfa Meem Saakin · Idghaam · Qalqala · Qalb · Idghaam Meem Saakin

مَفَازًا ۝ حَدَآئِقَ وَاَعْنَابًا ۝ وَّكَوَاعِبَ اَتْرَابًا ۝ وَّكَاْسًا

دِهَاقًا ۝ لَا يَسْمَعُوْنَ فِيْهَا لَغْوًا وَّلَا كِذَّابًا ۝ جَزَآءً مِّنْ رَّبِّكَ عَطَآءً

حِسَابًا ۝ رَّبِّ السَّمٰوٰتِ وَالْاَرْضِ وَمَا بَيْنَهُمَا الرَّحْمٰنِ لَا يَمْلِكُوْنَ

مِنْهُ خِطَابًا ۝ يَوْمَ يَقُوْمُ الرُّوْحُ وَالْمَلٰٓئِكَةُ صَفًّا ۚ لَا يَتَكَلَّمُوْنَ

اِلَّا مَنْ اَذِنَ لَهُ الرَّحْمٰنُ وَقَالَ صَوَابًا ۝ ذٰلِكَ الْيَوْمُ الْحَقُّ ۚ فَمَنْ

شَآءَ اتَّخَذَ اِلٰى رَبِّهٖ مَاٰبًا ۝ اِنَّا اَنْذَرْنٰكُمْ عَذَابًا قَرِيْبًا ۚ يَّوْمَ يَنْظُرُ

الْمَرْءُ مَا قَدَّمَتْ يَدٰهُ وَيَقُوْلُ الْكَافِرُ يٰلَيْتَنِيْ كُنْتُ تُرٰبًا ۝

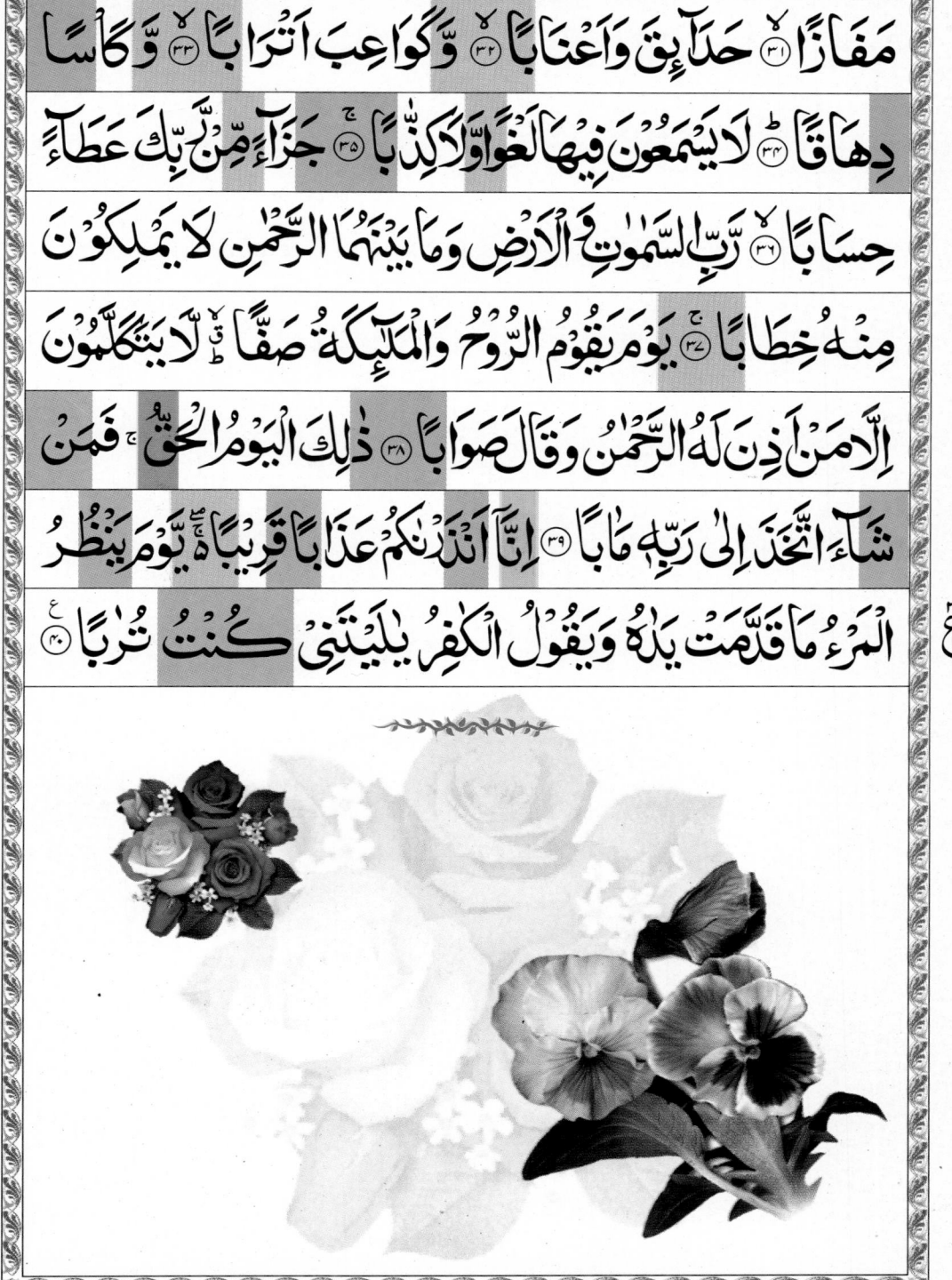

TAJWEED RULES
TO BE OBSERVED WHEN
RECITING
THE HOLY QUR'ÂN

أَحْكَامُ التَّجْوِيدِ الَّتِي تَجِبُ

مُرَاعَاتُهَا عِنْدَ تِلَاوَةِ الْقُرْآن

Compiled by
A Group of Islamic Scholars

JUZ'U'AMMA

(With Colour Coded Tajweed Rules in English)

First Edition: 2002

Reprint Edition: 2007-08

ISBN: 81-7231-420-5

Published by *Abdul Naeem for*

Islamic Book Service

2872-74 Kucha Chelan, Darya Ganj, New Delhi-110002 **(India)**
Ph.: 23253514, 23286551, 23244556, Fax:011-23277913
E-mail: Islamic@eth.net. Ibsdelhi@del2.vsnl.net.in
Website: www.islamic-india.com

Our Associates

Al Munna Book Shop Ltd.
Sharjah Tel.: 06-561-5483 & **Dubai Branch** Tel.:04-352-9294
E-mail: nusrat@emirates.net.ae

Azhar Academy Ltd
Continenta House, Cooks Road, London E15 2PW
Tel./Fax: 020 8534 9191, *E-mail:* sales@azharacademy.com

Printed in India

TABLE OF CONTENTS

THE AADAAB OF RECITING
THE HOLY QUR'ân

☐ The reciter of the Holy Qur'ân must perform the ritual ablution (wudhu).

☐ The intention when reciting the Holy Qur'ân should be to gain the pleasure of Allah.

☐ The voice should not be raised to such an extent where your recital will disturb others who are also engaged in some form of worship.

☐ The reciter of the Holy Qur'ân must sit in a dignified position facing the Ka'bah.

☐ When commencing with the recitation of the Holy Qur'ân – start by reciting:

" I seek Allah's protection from Satan, the accursed."

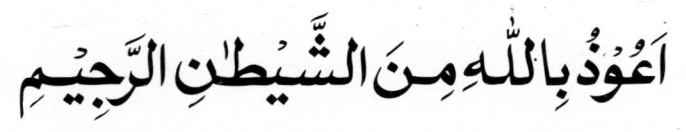

" I seek Allah's protection from Satan, the accursed."

And thereafter recite:

"In the name of Allah, Most Gracious, Most Merciful."

The place of origin (مَخْرَجٌ/مَخَارِجٌ)

of the Arabic letters

To know the origin of any letter of the Arabic Alphabet, place a Sukoon (ْ) on it and preceed it with an Alif (ا) with a Fatha (اَ).

Example : اَبْ will give us the origin of the letter بَ .

Name	Letter	Place of origin
The Aerial letters اَلْحُرُوْفُ الْهَوَائِيّةَ	ا و ي	Originate from the emptiness of the mouth.
The Guttural letters اَلْحُرُوْفُ الْحَلْقِيّةَ	ه	Originate from the back of the throat (larynx).
	ح ع	Originate from the centre of the throat.
	خ غ	Originate from the upper portion of the throat.
اَلْحَرْفَانِ اللَّهْوِيَانِ	ق ك	The back of the tongue rises and touches the soft palate.
اَلْحَرْفَانِ الشَّجْرِيَتَانِ	ج ش	The centre of the tongue touches the upper palate.

The letter ضَ اَلْحَرُفُ ضَ	ض	The upturned sides of the tongue touches the gums of the upper back teeth.
The liquids اَلْحُرُوْفُ الذُّوْلَقِيَّةِ	ر ل ن	Originate when the tip of the tongue touches the upper hard palate.
The dental letters اَلْحُرُوْفُ النِّطِيَّةَ	ت د ط	Originate when the tip of the tongue touches the gums of the upper two front teeth.
The gingieal letters اَلْحُرُوْفُ اللّثَوِيَّةِ	ث ذ ط	Originate when the tip of the tongue touches the edge of the upper two front teeth.
اَلْحُرُوْفُ الأَسَلِيَّةَ	ز س ص	Originate when the tip of the tongue rises towards the upper palate, touching the gums behind the upper two front teeth.
The labial letters اَلْحُرُوْفُ الشَّفَوِيَّةِ	ب م ف	Originate from the lips. Originates when the inner portion of the bottom lip meets the edge on the two upper front teeth.

TAJWEED

Reciting the Holy Qur'ân with TAJWEED means to pronounce every letter with all its articulative qualities such as the correct prolongation, merging, conversion, distinctness, and pauses. Reciting the Qur'ân with TAJWEED allows the reciter to emphasise the accent, phonetics, rhythm and temper of the Qur'ânic recitation.

QALQALA

When the letters of QALQALA have a Sukoon ( ) on it, it will be read with an echoing or jerking sound.

The letters of QALQALA are:

د	ج	ب	ط	ق

In the examples that follow, the QALQALA letter with a Sukoon appears in the red block. Care should be taken when reciting, not to jerk the letter to the extent where it will sound as if the letter has a FATHA on it.

Surah Number	Verse Number	Extract from Verse	Qalqala Letter
7	12	خَلَقْتَنِیْ مِنْ نَّارٍ وَّخَلَقْتَهٗ مِنْ	ق
37	10	خَطِفَ الْخَطْفَةَ فَاَتْبَعَهٗ شِهَابٌ ثَاقِبٌ	ط
2	34	قُلْنَا لِلْمَلٰٓئِكَةِ اسْجُدُوْا لِاٰدَمَ فَسَجَدُوْۤا اِلَّاۤ اِبْلِیْسَ	ب
37	19	فَاِنَّمَا هِیَ زَجْرَةٌ وَّاحِدَةٌ فَاِذَا هُمْ يَنْظُرُوْنَ	ج
33	4	جَعَلَ اَدْعِيَآءَكُمْ اَبْنَآءَكُمْ	د

When a stop is made at the end of the sentences below, the rule of QALQALA will apply. The last letter becomes SAAKIN irrespective of the vowel sign, thus resulting in the QALQALA letter being read with an echoing or jerking sound.

Surah Number	Verse Number	Extract from Verse	Qalqala Letter
37	5	وَمَا بَيْنَهُمَا وَرَبُّ الْمَشَارِقِ	ق
11	70	اِنَّآ اُرْسِلْنَآ اِلٰى قَوْمِ لُوطٍ	ط
37	10	خَطِفَ الْخَطْفَةَ فَاَتْبَعَهُ شِهَابٌ ثَاقِبٌ	ب
2	197	وَلَا فُسُوْقَ وَلَا جِدَالَ فِي الْحَجِّ	ج
37	7	وَحِفْظًا مِّنْ كُلِّ شَيْطٰنٍ مَّارِدٍ	د

NOON and MEEM MUSHADDADAH

When the letters ن and م have a SHADDAH (ّ) on it, (مّ نّ) it will be recited with Ghunna. The nazalization should not exceed the duration of two harakah. (2 - 3 second duration).

Surah Number	Verse Number	Extract from Verse	Mushaddadah Letter
37	6	اِنَّا زَيَّنَّا السَّمَآءَ الدُّنْيَا	نّ
78	21	اِنَّ جَهَنَّمَ كَانَتْ مِرْصَادًا	نّ
27	70	وَلَا تَكُنْ فِيْ ضَيْقٍ مِّمَّا يَمْكُرُوْنَ	مّ
7	11	وَلَقَدْ خَلَقْنٰكُمْ ثُمَّ صَوَّرْنٰكُمْ ثُمَّ قُلْنَا	مّ

THE RULE OF THE LETTER LAAM

When a letter with FATHA (◌َ) or DHAMMA (◌ُ) appears before the name of ALLAH, it will be pronounced with a broad sound or full mouth.

Surah Number	Verse Number	Extract from Verse	Vowel Sign
5	114	قَالَ عِيْسَى ابْنُ مَرْيَمَ اللّٰهُمَّ	◌َ
4	171	اِنَّمَا الْمَسِيْحُ عِيْسَى ابْنُ مَرْيَمَ رَسُوْلُ اللّٰهِ	◌ُ

When a letter with a KASRA (◌ِ) appears before the name of ALLAH, it will be pronounced with a thin sound or an empty mouth.

Surah Number	Verse Number	Extract from Verse	Vowel Sign
40	78	لِرَسُوْلٍ اَنْ يَّأْتِيَ بِاٰيَةٍ اِلَّا بِاِذْنِ اللّٰهِ	◌ِ
4	35	يُّوَفِّقِ اللّٰهُ بَيْنَهُمَا	◌ِ

However, the LAAM MUSHADDADAH لّ is read with a thin sound or empty mouth.

Surah Number	Verse Number	Extract from Verse	Laam Mushaddadah
2	255	اَللّٰهُ لَاۤ اِلٰهَ اِلَّا هُوَ اَلْحَيُّ الْقَيُّوْمُ	لّ
58	20	يُحَآدُّوْنَ اللّٰهَ وَرَسُوْلَهٗ اُولٰٓئِكَ فِي الْاَذَلِّيْنَ	
2	177	لَيْسَ الْبِرَّاَنْ تُوَلُّوْا وُجُوْهَكُمْ قِبَلَ	
2	148	وَلِكُلٍّ وِّجْهَةٌ هُوَ مُوَلِّيْهَا فَاسْتَبِقُوا	

THE RULE OF MEEM SAAKIN (مْ)

There are three rules regarding the MEEM SAAKIN مْ:
1. IKHFA SHAFAWI
2. IDGHAAM SHAFAWI
3. ITHAAR SHAFAWI

1. IKHFA SHAFAWI – MEEM SAAKIN

When the letter BA(ب) appears after a MEEM SAAKIN (مْ) there will be IKHFA SHAFAWI. It will be pronounced with a light nasal sound in the nose for a duration of 2 harakah. (2 - 3 second duration).

Surah Number	Verse Number	Extract from Verse	Ikhfa Shafawi Meem Saakin
34	8	اَفْتَرٰى عَلَى اللّٰهِ كَذِبًا اَمْ بِهٖ جِنَّةٌ	مْ ← ب

2. IDGHAAM SHAFAWI – MEEM SAAKIN

If after a MEEM SAAKIN (مْ) there appears a MEEM MUSHADDADAH (مّ), IDGHAAM will occur. In other words, the two MEEMS will become incorporated and be read with GHUNNA (nasalization).

Surah Number	Verse Number	Extract from Verse	Idghaam Shafawi Meem Saakin
16	57	وَلَهُمْ مَّا يَشْتَهُوْنَ	مْ ← مّ

3. ITHAAR SHAFAWI – MEEM SAAKIN

When after a MEEM SAAKIN (مْ) there appear any of the 26 letters other than the letters BA (ب) and MEEM (م), there will be ITHAAR SHAFAWI. No GHUNNA will occur.

Surah Number	Verse Number	Extract from Verse	Ithaar Shafawi Meem Saakin
34	45	وَكَذَّبَ الَّذِيْنَ مِنْ قَبْلِهِمْ وَمَا بَلَغُوْا	26 letters other than ب or م

IKHFA – NOON SAAKIN AND TANWEEN

If any of the 15 letters of IKHFA below come after a Noon Saakin (نْ) or Tanween (ٌ ٍ ً) the word must be read with a light nasal sound in the nose for a duration of two harakah. (2 - 3 second duration).

The letters of IKHFA are :

ش	س	ز	ذ	د	ج	ث	ت
ك	ق	ف	ظ	ط	ض	ص	

Surah Number	Verse Number	Extract from Verse	Ikhfa Letter
5	118	وَاِنْ تَغْفِرْ لَهُمْ فَاِنَّكَ	ت
5	119	لَهُمْ جَنَّتٌ تَجْرِىْ مِنْ تَحْتِهَا	
13	8	تَحْمِلُ كُلُّ اُنْثٰى وَمَا تَغِيْضُ الْاَرْحَامُ	ث
6	54	سُوْٓءًا بِجَهَالَةٍ ثُمَّ تَابَ مِنْ بَعْدِهٖ	
14	6	عَلَيْكُمْ اِذْ اَنْجٰىكُمْ مِّنْ اٰلِ	ج
14	19	يَأْتِ بِخَلْقٍ جَدِيْدٍ ۱۹	
14	22	اَنْ دَعَوْتُكُمْ فَاسْتَجَبْتُمْ لِيْ	د
6	99	وَمِنَ النَّخْلِ مِنْ طَلْعِهَا قِنْوَانٌ دَانِيَةٌ	
5	91	وَيَصُدَّكُمْ عَنْ ذِكْرِ اللّٰهِ وَعَنِ	ذ
3	185	كُلُّ نَفْسٍ ذَآئِقَةُ الْمَوْتِ	
3	185	فَمَنْ زُحْزِحَ عَنِ النَّارِ وَاُدْخِلَ الْجَنَّةَ	ز
18	74	نَفْسًا زَكِيَّةً بِغَيْرِ نَفْسٍ	

Surah Number	Verse Number	Extract from Verse	Ikhfa Letter
17	83	وَإِذَآ أَنْعَمْنَا عَلَى الْإِنْسَانِ	س
18	22	وَيَقُولُونَ خَمْسَةٌ سَادِسُهُمْ كَلْبُهُمْ	
18	69	قَالَ سَتَجِدُنِيۤ إِنْ شَآءَ اللهُ صَابِرًا	ش
17	58	عَذَابًا شَدِيدًا ۚ كَانَ ذَٰلِكَ فِى الْكِتٰبِ	
18	43	وَلَمْ تَكُنْ لَّهُ فِئَةٌ يَنْصُرُونَهُ	ص
33	23	مِنَ الْمُؤْمِنِينَ رِجَالٌ صَدَقُوا مَا	
30	54	اَللهُ الَّذِى خَلَقَكُمْ مِّنْ ضُعْفٍ	ض
30	54	بَعْدِ قُوَّةٍ ضُعْفًا وَّ شَيْبَةً	
32	7	مِنْ طِينٍ ۚ ثُمَّ جَعَلَ نَسْلَهُ مِنْ سُلٰلَةٍ	ط
34	15	بَلْدَةٌ طَيِّبَةٌ وَّ رَبٌّ غَفُورٌ	
35	44	اَوَلَمْ يَسِيرُوا فِى الْأَرْضِ فَيَنْظُرُوا كَيْفَ	ظ
4	57	وَنُدْخِلُهُمْ ظِلًّا ظَلِيلًا	
4	71	حِذْرَكُمْ فَانْفِرُوا ثُبَاتٍ اَوِ انْفِرُوا جَمِيعًا	ف
4	79	مَآ أَصَابَكَ مِنْ حَسَنَةٍ فَمِنَ اللهِ	
4	92	وَمَنْ قَتَلَ مُؤْمِنًا خَطَأً فَتَحْرِيرُ رَقَبَةٍ	ق
4	141	وَإِنْ كَانَ لِلْكٰفِرِينَ نَصِيبٌ قَالُوٓا	
4	141	فَإِنْ كَانَ لَكُمْ فَتْحٌ مِّنَ اللهِ	ك
4	31	سَيِّاٰتِكُمْ وَنُدْخِلْكُمْ مُّدْخَلًا كَرِيمًا	

ITHAAR – NOON SAAKIN AND TANWEEN

When after a NOON SAKIN (نْ) or TANWEEN (ـٌـٍـً) there appears any of the HUROOF HALQIYAH letters (throat letters) then it will be pronounced without GHUNNA (no nasalization).

The letters of HUROOF HALQIYAH are:

ه	ء	غ	ع	خ	ح

Surah Number	Verse Number	Extract from Verse	Huroof Halqiyah Letter
15	82 .	مُعْرِضِيْنَ ۞ وَكَانُوْا يَنْحِتُوْنَ	ح
2	35	وَكُلَا مِنْهَا رَغَدًا حَيْثُ شِئْتُمَا	
4	35	وَاِنْ خِفْتُمْ شِقَاقَ بَيْنِهِمَا فَابْعَثُوْا	خ
4	35	اِنَّ اللهَ كَانَ عَلِيْمًا خَبِيْرًا ۞	
6	54	نَفْسِهِ الرَّحْمَةَ ۛ اَنَّهُ مَنْ عَمِلَ مِنْكُمْ	ع
6	54	بِاٰيٰتِنَا فَقُلْ سَلٰمٌ عَلَيْكُمْ كَتَبَ	
7	43	فِيْ صُدُوْرِهِمْ مِّنْ غِلٍّ تَجْرِيْ مِنْ	غ
35	28	اِنَّ اللهَ عَزِيْزٌ غَفُوْرٌ ۞	
5	32	مِنْ اَجْلِ ذٰلِكَ ۚ	ء / أ
38	29	كِتٰبٌ اَنْزَلْنٰهُ اِلَيْكَ مُبٰرَكٌ لِّيَدَّبَّرُوْا	
3	104	وَيَأْمُرُوْنَ بِالْمَعْرُوْفِ وَيَنْهَوْنَ	ه
13	7	اَنْتَ مُنْذِرٌ وَّلِكُلِّ قَوْمٍ هَادٍ ۞	

IDGHAAM – NOON SAAKIN AND TANWEEN

IDGHAAM refers to the assimilation of one letter into the other. The rule of IDGHAAM will apply when the letters و م ن ي is preceded by a NOON SAAKIN (نْ) or TANWEEN (ـًـٍـٌ). The emphasis will be on the succeeding letter because of the presence of a SHADDAH (ّ) and will be read with GHUNNA. The nasalization should not exceed the duration of two harakah. (2 - 3 second duration).

Surah Number	Verse Number	Extract from Verse	Surah Number	Verses Number	Extract from Verse	Idghaam Letter
13	23	عَدْنٍ يَّدْخُلُوْنَهَا	18	5	اِنْ يَّقُوْلُوْنَ	ي
13	27	اٰيَةٌ مِّنْ رَّبِّهٖ	2	130	عَنْ مِّلَّةِ	م
15	45	جَنّٰتٍ وَّعُيُوْنٍ	13	11	مِنْ وَّالٍ	و
14	44	قَرِيْبٍ نَّجِبْ	14	11	لَنَاۤ اَنْ تَأْتِيَكُمْ	ن

With regard to the letters LAAM (ل) and RAA (ر) the IDGHAAM will be without GHUNNA, but assimilation takes place.

Surah Number	Verse Number	Extract from Verse	Surah Number	Verse Number	Extract from Verse	Idghaam Letter
2	2	هُدًى لِّلْمُتَّقِيْنَ	36	47	مَنْ لَّوْ يَشَآءُ اللّٰهُ	ل
2	173	غَفُوْرٌ رَّحِيْمٌ	2	5	هُدًى مِّنْ رَّبِّهِمْ	ر

In the examples below, assimilation will not take place due to a lack of a SHADDAH (ّ) on the IDGHAAM letters.

Surah Number	Verse Number	Extract from Verse	Surah Number	Verse Number	Extract from Verse	Idghaam Letter
61	4	كَاَنَّهُمْ بُنْيَانٌ	30	7	الْحَيٰوةِ الدُّنْيَا	ي
6	99	طَلْعِهَا قِنْوَانٌ	13	4	نَخِيْلٌ صِنْوَانٌ	و

IDGHAAM MITHLAYN
(Assimilation of the same kind)

This rule applies when two letters following each other are the same. The first letter has a SAAKIN (ْ) and the second letter is vocal and has a SHADDAH (ّ) on it. When reciting the letters keep in mind that the SAAKIN letter becomes assimilated into the letter following it.

Surah Number	Verse Number	Extract from Verse	Surah Number	Verse Number	Extract from Verse
4	78	يُدْرِكْكُّمُ	2	16	رَبِحَتْ تِّجَارَتُهُمْ
18	78	مَا لَمْ تَسْتَطِعْ عَّلَيْهِ	5	61	وَقَدْ دَّخَلُوْا
8	72	اٰوَوْا وَّ نَصَرُوْٓا	21	87	اِذْ ذَّهَبَ مُغَاضِبًا

IDGHAAM MUTAQAARIBAYN
(Assimilation of letters with similar origin)

This rule applies when a letter in a word is SAAKIN (ْ) and the letter following it has a SHADDAH (ّ). When pronounced appears to be close to the same place of origin as the SAAKIN letter. The SAAKIN letter will assimilate with the vocal letter when recited.

Surah Number	Verse Number	Extract from Verse	Few examples to illustrate Idghaam Mutaqaaribayn	
77	20	نَخْلُقْكُّمْ مِّنْ مَّآءٍ مَّهِيْنٍ ﴿٢٠﴾	ك	ق
11	42	يٰبُنَيَّ ارْكَبْ مَّعَنَا	م	ب
17	80	وَقُلْ رَّبِّ اَدْخِلْنِيْ مُدْخَلَ	ر	ل
20	49	فَمَنْ رَّبُّكُمَا يٰمُوْسٰى ﴿٤٩﴾	ر	ن

IDGHAAM MUTAJAANISAYN
(Assimilation of related kind)

This rule applies when a letter in a word is SAAKIN (ْ) and the letter following it has a SHADDAH (ّ) and when pronounced has the same place of origin as the SAAKIN letter. The SAAKIN letter will assimilate with the vocal letter when recited.

Surah Number	Verse Number	Extract from Verse	Few examples to illustrate Idghaam Mutajaanisayn
5	28	لَئِنۢ بَسَطتَّ اِلَيَّ يَدَكَ	ت \ ط
10	89	قَالَ قَدۡ اُجِيبَت دَّعۡوَتُكُمَا	ت \ د
4	64	اَنَّهُمۡ اِذ ظَّلَمُوٓا اَنۡفُسَهُمۡ	ذ \ ظ
3	72	وَقَالَت طَّآئِفَةٌ مِّنۡ اَهۡلِ	ت \ ط

IQLAAB – The Alteration (Noon Saakin and Tanween)

When after a NOON SAAKIN (نْ) or Tanween (ـًـٍـٌ) the letter BA (ب) appears then the NOON SAAKIN or TANWEEN will become substituted by a small MEEM SAAKIN (مْ) and will be recited with GHUNNA.

Surah Number	Verse Number	Extract from Verse
2	27	عَهۡدَ اللّٰهِ مِنۢ بَعۡدِ
2	181	فَمَنۢ بَدَّلَهٗ
2	18	صُمٌّ بُكۡمٌ عُمۡىٌ
2	282	فُسُوقٌۢ بِكُمۡ

The letter RAA

1. A RAA (ر) with a FATHA (ﹷ) or DHAMMA (ﹹ) on it should be pronounced with a full mouth.

Surah Number	Verse Number	Extract from Verse	The Letter
2	16	فَمَا رَبِحَت تِّجَارَتُهُم	رَ
2	28	تَكۡفُرُوۡنَ بِاللّٰهِ وَكُنۡتُمۡ	رُ

2. A RAA (ر) with a KASRA (ﹻ) should be pronounced with an empty mouth.

Surah Number	Verse Number	Extract from Verse	The Letter
2	54	تَكُمۡ عِنۡدَ بَارِیِٕكُمۡ	رِ
2	75	كَلٰمَ اللّٰهِ ثُمَّ يُحَرِّفُوۡنَهٗ	رِ

3. When a FATHA (ﹷ) or DHAMMA (ﹹ) appear before a RAA SAAKIN (رْ) the letter RAA SAAKIN (رْ) will be pronounced with a full mouth.

Surah Number	Verse Number	Extract from Verse	The Letter Raa Saakin
2	7	اَبۡيَامٍ وَّكَانَ عَرۡشُهٗ عَلَى	ﹷ رْ
2	252	وَاِنَّكَ لَمِنَ الۡمُرۡسَلِيۡنَ	ﹹ رْ

4. If a KASRA (ﹻ) appears before a RAA SAAKIN (رْ) the RAA SAAKIN (رْ) will be read with an empty mouth.

Surah Number	Verse Number	Extract from Verse	The Letter Raa Saakin
2	6	تُنۡذِرۡهُمۡ لَا يُؤۡمِنُوۡنَ	ﹻ رْ

5. If a SHADDAH (ّ) appears on the letter RAA (رّ) and has either a FATHA (َ) or DHAMMA (ُ) it will be pronounced with a full mouth.

Surah Number	Verse Number	Extract from Verse	Raa with a Shaddah
2	177	لَيْسَ الْبِرَّ اَنْ تُوَلُّوْا وُجُوْهَكُمْ قِبَلَ	رّ
18	36	قَآئِمَةًۙ وَّلَئِنْ رُّدِدْتُّ	رّ

6. If a SHADDAH (ّ) appears on the letter RAA (ر) and has a KASRA (ِ) it will be pronounced with an empty mouth.

Surah Number	Verse Number	Extract from Verse	Raa with a Shaddah
113	2	مِنْ شَرِّ مَا خَلَقَ ۙ	رّ
6	97	بِهَا فِيْ ظُلُمٰتِ الْبَرِّ وَالْبَحْرِ	رّ

7. When a YAA SAAKIN (يْ) appears before a RAA MOUQUF and the letter preceding the YAA SAAKIN has a KASRA (ِ) then the RAA (ر) will be recited with an empty mouth.

Surah Number	Verse Number	Extract from Verse	يْ preceeded by a Kasra	
3	180	بِمَا تَعْمَلُوْنَ خَبِيْرٌ	يْ	ِ
34	12	نُذِقْهُ مِنْ عَذَابِ السَّعِيْرِ	يْ	ِ
17	1	اِنَّهٗ هُوَ السَّمِيْعُ الْبَصِيْرُ	يْ	ِ
3	184	وَالزُّبُرِ وَالْكِتٰبِ الْمُنِيْرِ	يْ	ِ

8. When a letter other than a YAA SAAKIN (يْ) appears before a RAA MAUQUF, and the letter has a SUKOON (ْ) on it and the letter preceding it has either a FATHA (َ) or DHAMMA (ُ) on it then the RAA (ر) with be recited with a full mouth.

Surah Number	Verse Number	Extract from Verse	Letter preceded by a Fatha/Dhamma	
103	3	وَتَوَاصَوْا بِالْحَقِّ ۛ وَتَوَاصَوْا بِالصَّبْرِ	ب	َ
103	2	إِنَّ الْإِنْسَانَ لَفِي خُسْرٍ	س	ُ

The MADD – Elongation

The HUROOFUL MADD letters are:

ا   و   ي

MADDUL ASLI – The Original
Elongation of 2 Harakah (Qasr – shortness)

ALIF (ا) is one of the letters of MADD when it is preceded by a FATHA (َ).

WAW (و) is one of the letters of MADD when it is preceded by a DHAMMA (ُ).

YAA (ي) is one of the letters of MADD when it is preceded by a KASRA (ِ).

Surah Number	Verse Number	Extract from Verse	Hurooful Madd Letter
2	71	قَالَ إِنَّهُ يَقُولُ إِنَّهَا	ا
2	26	الَّذِينَ كَفَرُوا فَيَقُولُونَ مَاذَا أَرَادَ اللهُ	و
2	90	وَلِلْكَافِرِينَ عَذَابٌ مُهِينٌ	ي

MADDUL MUTTASIL ~
(The Joined Elongation)

When a HUROOFUL MADD letter (ا و ي) is followed by a HAMZA (ء) in the same word, the MADD is known as MADDUL MUTTASIL.

The length of recitation of the MADDUL MUTTASIL will be TOOL (lengthy). i.e. 4 to 6 HARAKAAT long. (4 - 6 second duration).

Surah Number	Verse Number	Extract from Verse	Surah Number	Verse Number	Extract from Verse	Hurowith Madd Letter
2	6	سَوَآءٌ عَلَيْهِمْ	110	1	إِذَا جَآءَ نَصْرُ	ا
13	25	سُوٓءُ الدَّارِ	4	110	سُوٓءًا أَوْ يَظْلِمْ	و
89	23	وَجِآىْءَ يَوْمَئِذٍ	4	4	هَنِيٓئًا مَّرِيٓئًا	ي

MADDUL MUNFASIL ~
(The Detached Elongation)

If a word ends in one of the HUROOFUL MADD letters (ي و ا) and the following word begins with a HAMZA (ء / ا) then that MADD is known as MADDUL MUNFASIL. The length of recitation of the MADDUL MUNFASIL will be TAWASSUT (intermediate).
i.e. 3 to 5 HARAKAAT long. (3 -5 second duration).

Surah Number	Verse Number	Extract from Verse	Surah Number	Verse Number	Extract from Verse	Huroful Madd Letter
97	1	إِنَّآ أَنْزَلْنٰهُ	108	1	إِنَّآ أَعْطَيْنٰكَ	ا
2	235	وَاعْلَمُوٓا أَنَّ اللَّهَ	66	6	قُوٓا أَنْفُسَكُمْ	و
4	135	وَلَوْ عَلَىٰٓ أَنْفُسِكُمْ	51	21	وَفِيٓ أَنْفُسِكُمْ	ي

MADDUL LAAZIM ~
(The Compulsory Elongation)

It is imperative to pronounce the HUROOF MUQATTA 'AAT letters which appear at the beginning of a SURAH. This MADD is called MADDUL LAAZIM. The length of recitation of MADDUL LAAZIM will be TOOL (lengthy). I.e. 6 HARAKAAT long. (6 second duration).

Surah Number	Verse Number	Huroof Muqatta 'aat	Surah Number	Verses Number	Huroof Muqatta 'aat
50	1	قٓ ۚ وَالْقُرْاٰنِ الْمَجِيْدِ ۚ	19	1	كٰهٰيٰعٓصٓ ۚ
45	1	حٰمٓ ۚ تَنْزِيْلُ	68	1	نٓ وَالْقَلَمِ وَمَا
42	2	حٰمٓ ۚ عٓسٓقٓ ۚ	2	1	الٓمٓ ۚ

MADDUL AARIDH
(The Abrupt Stop Elongation)

If after any HUROOFUL MADD letter (ا و ي) there appears a SAAKIN which is caused by a WAQAF (stop) then such a MADD is known as MADDUL AARIDH. The length of recitation of the MADDUL AARIDH will be TAWASSUT (intermediate). i.e. 2 to 5 HARAKAAT long. (2-5 second duration).

Surah Number	Verse Number	Extract from Verse	Hurooful Madd Letter
46	32	مِنْ دُوْنِهٖٓ اَوْلِيَآءُ	ا
67	27	هٰذَا الَّذِيْ كُنْتُمْ بِهٖ تَدَّعُوْنَ ۞	و
19	37	مِنْ مَّشْهَدِ يَوْمٍ عَظِيْمٍ ۞	ي

THE SUN LETTER

When the definite article (اَلْ) is attached to an indefinite word, the TANWEEN (ـٌـٍـً) changes into a short vowel, eg. اَلشَّجَرَةُ   شَجَرَةٌ .

An indefinite word, eg. شَجَرَةٌ beginning with a SUN LETTER and with the definite article (اَلْ) attached to it, (اَلشَّجَرَةُ) results in the LAAM (ل) not being pronounced.

The ALIF (ا) in the definite article (ال) is recited and merges with the SUN LETTER which now has a SHADDAH (ّ) on it when recited, eg. اَلشَّجَرَةُ .

The SHADDAH (ّ) sign is an indication that the pronunciation must be hardened,

However, if the definite article (ال) is preceded by a word or letter then it will not be pronounced, eg. تَحْتَ الشَّجَرَةِ

The sun letters are:

س	ز	ر	ذ	د	ث	ت
ن	ل	ظ	ط	ض	ص	ش

Surah Number	Verse Number	Definite article preceded by letter/word	Definite article attached to word	Sun Letter
95	1	وَالتِّيْنِ	التِّيْنِ	ت
3	195	حُسْنُ الثَّوَابِ ۹۵	الثَّوَابِ ۹۵	ث
1	3	يَوْمِ الدِّيْنِ ۳	الدِّيْنِ ۳	د
51	1	وَالذَّارِيٰتِ	الذَّارِيٰتِ	ذ
2	143	وَيَكُوْنَ الرَّسُوْلُ	الرَّسُوْلُ	ر
2	277	وَاٰتَوُا الزَّكٰوةَ	الزَّكٰوةَ	ز
2	22	مِنَ السَّمَآءِ	السَّمَآءِ	س
25	29	وَكَانَ الشَّيْطٰنُ	الشَّيْطٰنُ	ش
112	2	اَللّٰهُ الصَّمَدُ ۲	الصَّمَدُ ۲	ص
9	91	عَلَى الضُّعَفَآءِ	الضُّعَفَآءِ	ض
2	260	مِّنَ الطَّيْرِ	الطَّيْرِ	ط
4	75	هٰذِهِ الْقَرْيَةِ الظَّالِمِ	الظَّالِمِ	ظ
2	274	بِالَّيْلِ	الَّيْلِ	ل
75	2	بِالنَّفْسِ	النَّفْسِ	ن

THE MOON LETTER

When the definite article (اَلْ) is attached to an indefinite word, the TANWEEN (ـٌـٍ) changes into a short vowel eg. مَسْجِدٌ الْمَسْجِدُ

An indefinite word, eg. مَسْجِدٌ beginning with a MOON LETTER and with the definite article (اَلْ) attached to it, (الْمَسْجِدُ) results in the LAAM (ل) being pronounced as a LAAM SAAKIN (لْ). The ALIF (ا) in the definite article becomes HAMZA TUL WASL i.e. the ALIF (ا) is written, but is not pronounced when a word or letter precedes it eg. فِى الْمَسْجِدِ . However, if the definite noun (الْمَسْجِدُ) appears as the first word in a sentence then the ALIF will be pronounced.

The MOON letters are:

ح	ج	ب	أ
ف	غ	ع	خ
و	م	كـ	ق
	ي	هـ	

Surah Number	Verse Number	Definite article preceded by letter/word	Definite article attached to word	Moon Letter
12	6	تَأْوِيلِ الْأَحَادِيثِ	الْأَحَادِيثِ	أ
2	127	مِنَ الْبَيْتِ	الْبَيْتِ	ب
7	40	يَلِجَ الْجَمَلُ	الْجَمَلُ	ج
69	2	مَا الْحَاقَّةُ	الْحَاقَّةُ	ح
52	35	أَمْ هُمُ الْخَالِقُونَ	الْخَالِقُونَ	خ
10	88	يَرَوُا الْعَذَابَ	الْعَذَابَ	ع
10	90	أَدْرَكَهُ الْغَرَقُ	الْغَرَقُ	غ
2	191	وَالْفِتْنَةُ	الْفِتْنَةُ	ف
16	107	لَا يَهْدِى الْقَوْمَ	الْقَوْمَ	ق
18	9	أَصْحَبَ الْكَهْفِ	الْكَهْفِ	ك
1	7	غَيْرِ الْمَغْضُوبِ	الْمَغْضُوبِ	م
56	1	وَقَعَتِ الْوَاقِعَةُ	الْوَاقِعَةُ	و
56	55	شُرْبَ الْهِيمِ	الْهِيمِ	ه
15	99	يَأْتِيَكَ الْيَقِينُ	الْيَقِينُ	ي

THE RULES OF STOPPING

If any of these signs (ﹷ ﹷ ﹷ) (ﹷ ﹷ ﹷ) appear on the last letter of a word when a stop is required, then the last letter is with a SAAKIN.

Surah Number	Verse Number	Extract from Verse	Surah Number	Verse Number	Extract from Verse
88	4	نَارًا حَامِيَةً ۝	15	8	إِذًا مُّنظَرِينَ ۝
7	24	إِلَىٰ حِينٍ ۝	88	1	حَدِيثُ الْغَاشِيَةِ ۝
15	6	إِنَّكَ لَمَجْنُونٌ ۝	89	27	النَّفْسُ الْمُطْمَئِنَّةُ ۝

However, if the last letter has a FATHATAAN or MADD then the last letter is read as if it has a FATHA on it.

Surah Number	Verse Number	Extract from Verse	Surah Number	Verse Number	Extract from Verse
78	28	بِآيَاتِنَا كِذَّابًا ۝	92	16	كَذَّبَ وَتَوَلَّىٰ ۝
79	19	رَبِّكَ فَتَخْشَىٰ ۝	89	20	حُبًّا جَمًّا ۝
79	2	وَالنَّاشِطَاتِ نَشْطًا ۝	91	1	وَالشَّمْسِ وَضُحَاهَا ۝

SYMBOLS DENOTING PAUSES

Compulsory stop

Surah Number	Verse Number	Extract from Verse	Symbol
19	16	وَاذْكُرْ فِى الْكِتٰبِ مَرْيَمَ اِذِ انْتَبَذَتْ	مـ

Necessary stop

Surah Number	Verse Number	Extract from Verse	Symbol
18	8	عَلَيْهَا صَعِيْدًا جُرُزًا ٨	ط

Stop vocal sound for a moment without breaking the breath

Surah Number	Verse Number	Extract from Verse	Symbol
2	286	وَاعْفُ عَنَّا وَاغْفِرْ لَنَا وَارْحَمْنَا اَنْتَ	وقفة
83	14	كَلَّا بَلْ رَانَ	سكتة

Necessary to continue, do not pause

Surah Number	Verse Number	Extract from Verse	Symbol
20	14	فَاعْبُدْنِيْ وَاَقِمِ الصَّلٰوةَ لِذِكْرِيْ	لا

Desirable to continue, do not pause

Surah Number	Verse Number	Extract from Verse	Symbol
18	24	اِلَّا اَنْ يَّشَاءَ اللهُ وَاذْكُرْ رَّبَّكَ	ز
19	17	حِجَابًا فَاَرْسَلْنَا اِلَيْهَا رُوْحَنَا	ص
18	4/5	قَالُوا اتَّخَذَ اللهُ وَلَدًا مَا لَهُمْ بِهِ	ق
18	13/14	وَزِدْنٰهُمْ هُدًى وَّرَبَطْنَا	صلی

Recommended pause

Surah Number	Verse Number	Extract from Verse	Symbol
2	285	وَمَلٰٓئِكَتِهِ وَكُتُبِهِ وَرُسُلِهِ لَا نُفَرِّقُ	قف

Optional to pause or to continue

Surah Number	Verse Number	Extract from Verse	Symbol
18	27	رَبِّكَ لَا مُبَدِّلَ لِكَلِمٰتِهِ وَلَنْ	ج

Any two of the three verses may be read in continuity

Surah Number	Verse Number	Extract from Verse	Symbol
25	32	وَقَالَ الَّذِيْنَ كَفَرُوْا لَوْلَا نُزِّلَ عَلَيْهِ الْقُرْاٰنُ جُمْلَةً وَّاحِدَةً كَذٰلِكَ لِنُثَبِّتَ بِهِ فُؤَادَكَ وَرَتَّلْنٰهُ تَرْتِيْلًا	⋮

PROSTRATION IS TO BE MADE WHEN RECITING ANY OF THE FOLLOWING VERSES.

Page Number	Surah Number	Verse Number	Extract from Verse	Sajda Number
247	7	206	وَيُسَبِّحُوْنَهٗ وَلَهٗ يَسْجُدُوْنَ ۩	1
351	13	15	وَلِلّٰهِ يَسْجُدُ مَنْ فِى السَّمٰوٰتِ وَالْاَرْضِ	2
381	16	49	وَلِلّٰهِ يَسْجُدُ مَا فِى السَّمٰوٰتِ وَمَا	3
410	17	107	لِلْاَذْقَانِ سُجَّدًا ۩ وَّيَقُوْلُوْنَ سُبْحٰنَ	4
433	19	58	اٰيٰتُ الرَّحْمٰنِ خَرُّوْا سُجَّدًا وَّبُكِيًّا ۩	5
467	22	18	اَلَمْ تَرَ اَنَّ اللّٰهَ يَسْجُدُ لَهٗ	6
511	25	60	وَاِذَا قِيْلَ لَهُمُ اسْجُدُوْا لِلرَّحْمٰنِ قَالُوْا	7
530	27	25	اَلَّا يَسْجُدُوْا لِلّٰهِ الَّذِيْ يُخْرِجُ الْخَبْءَ	8
581	32	15	خَرُّوْا سُجَّدًا وَّسَبَّحُوْا بِحَمْدِ رَبِّهِمْ	9
632	38	24	وَخَرَّ رَاكِعًا وَّاَنَابَ ۩	10
667	41	37	لَا تَسْجُدُوْا لِلشَّمْسِ وَلَا لِلْقَمَرِ وَاسْجُدُوْا	11
738	53	62	فَاسْجُدُوْا لِلّٰهِ وَاعْبُدُوْا ۩	12
831	84	21	لَا يَسْجُدُوْنَ ۩ بَلِ الَّذِيْنَ كَفَرُوْا يُكَذِّبُوْنَ	13
842	96	19	كَلَّا لَا تُطِعْهُ وَاسْجُدْ وَاقْتَرِبْ ۩	14

NOTES